Kusudama Origami

Making Awesome Origami Kusudama Papers

Table of Contents

Origami Kusudama Paper _______________ 1

What is the Kusudama ? _______________ 3

How to make a Kusudama Orgami _______ 5

Creating a Kusudama Ball _____________ 11

Rainbow Origami Kusudama Ball Mobile _ 22

Modular Origami Seasonal Ornament ____ 31

What is the Kusudama ?

The Japanese kusudama (薬玉; lit. medicine ball) is a paper model that is usually (although not always) created by sewing multiple identical pyramidal units (usually stylized flowers folded from square paper) together through their points to form a spherical shape. Alternately the individual components may be glued together. (e.g. the kusudama in the lower photo is entirely glued, not threaded together) Occasionally, a tassel is attached to the bottom for decoration.

Kusudama originate from ancient Japanese culture, where they were used for incense and potpourri; possibly originally being actual bunches of flowers or herbs. The word itself is a combination of two Japanese words *kusuri*, Medicine, and *tama*, Ball. They are now typically used as decorations, or as gifts.

The kusudama is important in origami particularly as a precursor to the modular origami genre. It is often confused with modular origami, but is not such because the units are strung or pasted together, instead of folded together as most modular construction are made.

It is, however, still considered origami, although origami purists frown upon using its characteristic technique of threading or gluing the units together, while others recognize that early traditional Japanese origami often used both cutting (see thousand origami cranes or senbazuru) and pasting, and respect kusudama as an ingenious traditional paper folding craft in the origami family.

Modern origami masters such as Tomoko Fuse have created new kusudama designs that are entirely assembled without cutting, glue or thread except as a hanger.

How to make a Kusudama Orgami

When learning how to fold origami flowers, you'll definitely want to add the kusudama flower to your list of projects. This pretty flower is relatively simple to fold but sure to impress all of your friends. Kusudama origami is made of several identically folded units that are glued together or sewn together to make a spherical shape. Kusudama is often considered a precursor to the modern genre of modular origami.

To make the kusudama flower, you can use origami paper, scrapbook paper, or calendar papers cut to the size you wish. Bigger paper results in bigger petals, which gives you a more dramatic looking flower. Mix and match patterns for an artistic effect or make all of the petals the same solid color if you want your flower to look as realistic as possible.

Children ages 6 and up should be able to fold the kusudama petal with a bit of practice, but will likely require adult assistance to make the completed flower. If you're folding this model with a child, use large 6-inch by 6-inch squares to make the project easiest for tiny hands to work with. You can also make a kusudama flower with money.

What You'll Need

- Equipment / Tools

- Paper clips (optional)
- Materials
- 6 sheets square paper
- Glue

Instructions

1. Form a Triangle

   Place the paper in front of you with the back side facing up. Fold it diagonally to make a triangle. In origami, this is sometimes called a shawl fold, diaper fold, or triangle fold. It is a simple base that is used to develop many different types of projects.

2. Make a Square

Fold the left and right corners up to the middle to make a square. In origami, this shape is called a helmet base.

> ➢ Tip
>
> Remember to make crisp folds to ensure the nicest-looking origami kusudama flower.

3. Fold the Corners Down

Fold the left and right corners down to meet the edge of the paper.

4. Flatten the Flaps

Flatten the flaps you created in the previous step. In origami, this is called a squash fold. Flattening without wrinkling the paper takes a bit of practice; however, the squash fold is one of the most important origami folds to know, as it is used in everything from origami flowers to origami cards. Fold the top triangles down.

5. Create Your Kusudama Flower Petals

Fold the left corner in, so it meets the first side crease. Repeat with the right corner. Carefully glue your flower petal together. Repeat until you have a total of six flower petals. Compare the flower petals when you are finished to make sure they are all exactly the same size and shape.

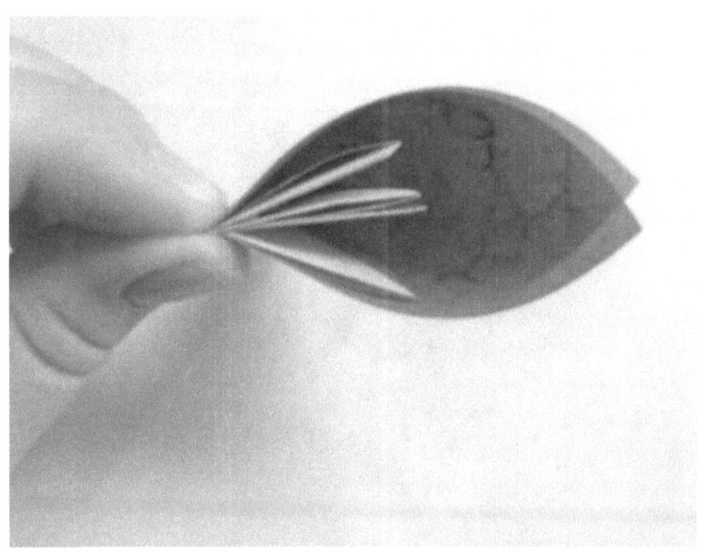

6. Complete Your Origami Kusudama Flower

Glue the petals together to form your kusudama origami flower. For best results, use a glue stick or liquid craft glue and let each connection dry before continuing. If you're having trouble, use paper clips on the middle of the petals to hold the flower together until all the glue is dry.

> ➤ Tip
>
> If you'd like to add a little extra embellishment to your kusudama flower, consider attaching a button, scrapbook brad, or rhinestone to the center. If you make a wire loop and thread your button through, you can use the excess wire to attach your flower to the bow on a beautifully wrapped package.

Creating a Kusudama Ball

If desired, you can fold 12 of the flowers and glue them together to make one large origami kusudama ball.

Making an Origami Bouquet

A single origami kusudama flower is pretty on its own, but kusudama flowers can also be added to origami bouquets to create pretty flower arrangements for weddings and other special occasions.

These charming origami flower balls have a history of being used for potpourri and incense in ancient Japan. Learn how to build your own kusudama with this easy-to-follow tutorial!

You will need:

- 60 squares of origami paper, cut square (mine are 3" x 3")
- Craft glue
- Paper clips or mini clothespins

I used a roll of shoji-gami rice paper, which you can find at art supply stores and on Amazon. The paper has a fine, fibrous texture, with a satiny finish on the surface. It felt just that little bit more special.

Instruction

1. Creating The Flower Petals

- Set out five pieces of paper. Each piece = 1 petal, and I find it faster to make all five petals at once.

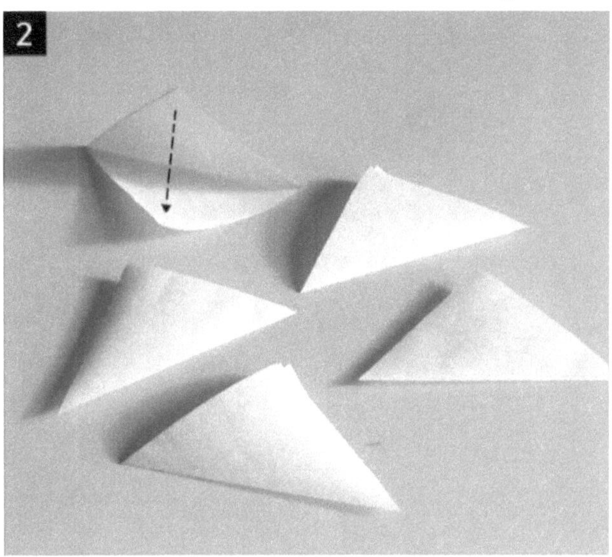

- Fold each piece of paper on the diagonal to make triangles.

- Fold the outer corners of the triangle up towards the center corner, making squares. (They should look like little fortune cookies.)

- Fold each flap in half, making little wings. The bottom edges should line up.

- Pull each wing taut, and then flatten along the center seam, making diamond shapes.

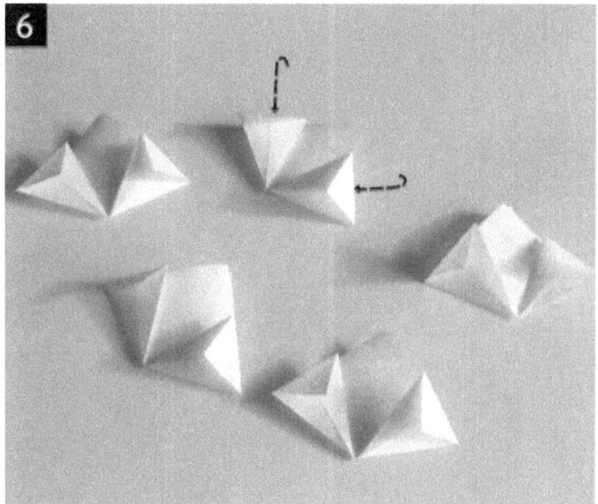

- Fold the tips of each diamond inwards. Again, these folds should be flush with the outer edges.

- Fold the flaps in half, along the center seam. Flatten the folded creases with your thumbnail or the side of a pen.

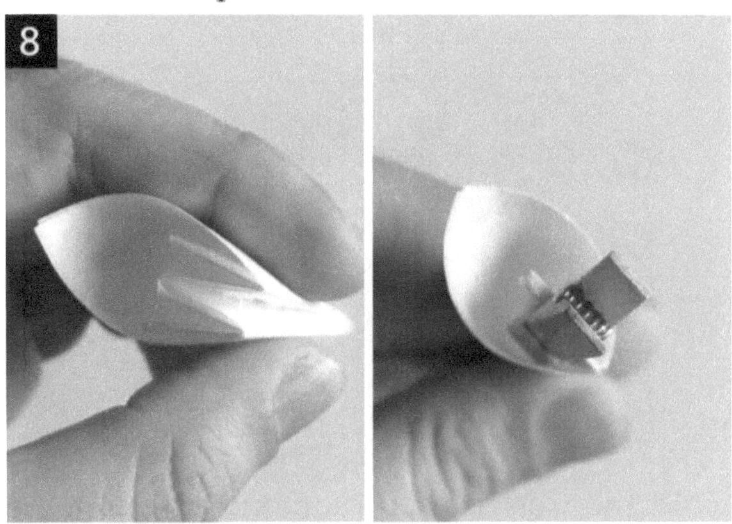

- Dab a bit of glue on the outside of the two flaps, then fold into a cone shape so that the flaps meet. Temporarily hold the center in place with a paper clip or (as shown here) a mini clothespin, until the glue dries.

2. Five of these petals will make each flower.

3. Assembling Each Flower

Apply a line of glue to the long center seam of two petals, glue them together, and then continue to glue in the rest, one by one. Boom, kusudama flower! Make twelve of these in order to create a flower ball.

4. Assembling The Kusudama

Once you have twelve flowers, you can make the kusudama ball. The ball is made from two halves of six flowers.

Apply a line of glue to the backs of two adjacent petals on one flower, do the same to a second, and then glue together using paper clips or mini pins. Look at the image here to see where the flowers were glued; the petals should line up with each other. Continue to glue flowers together in this manner – five will fit in the circle.

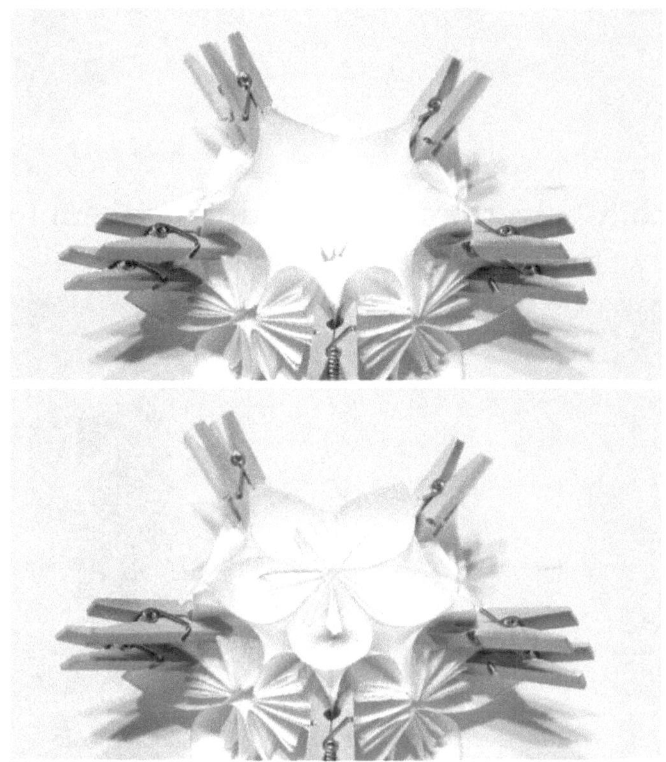

The sixth flower will fit in the hollow left by the other five. Glue it, clip it and you've made one half of the ball!

Once both halves are assembled, glue them together and leave the glue to dry overnight. That's it!

I love the delicate nature of my kusudama. The rice paper makes it soft, closer to actual flower petals. I tested out a few other flowers using other materials, like colored cardstock. These were harder to fold, but the end result is SOLID.

Rainbow Origami Kusudama Ball Mobile

Kusudama (medicine balls) are paper models made from smaller folded paper models that have been stitched or glued together. They are traditional and date back a number of years, with a great many different variations of flowers and geometric shapes used to form the ball itself. We decided to create a beautiful rainbow flower one to hang from our ceiling and brighten up our space, and to introduce some of our younger makerspace members to modular origami and to paper folding generally. The folds are super-easy to pick up and you can create a stunning artwork with a few sheets of paper, some glue, and not as much time as you'd think!

You will need:

- Origami paper squares: 10 sheets each of 6 different rainbow colours. You *can* use regular paper, but because it will be thicker, it will be trickier to work with and to keep looking neat. The squares can be any size you like (obviously the bigger the squares, the bigger the finished mobile) but they must be *exactly* square and *exactly* the same size!

- Paper Glue. We have found that PVA is a little messy and takes time to dry, but is strong. If you use glue sticks, ideally use extra strong ones.

- Clothes pegs, to hold bits of paper in place while they dry

- If you wish to hang your mobile, some ribbon or similar and a hole punch

Step 1: Fold Petals Part 1

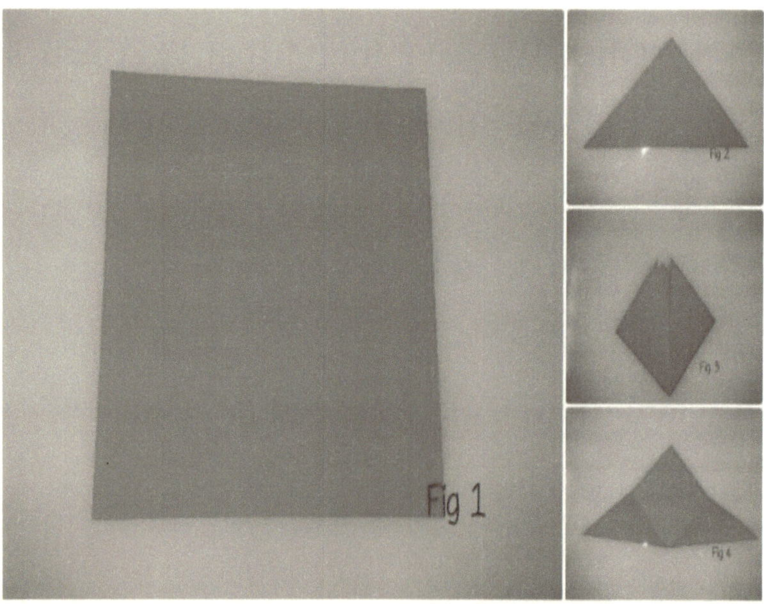

- The ball is made from 12 identical flowers. Each flower is made from 5 sheets of origami paper. Each sheet of paper is folded in exactly the same way before being glued. It seems a little complicated at first, but once you get the hang of it, it is quick and easy and you will be able to make them without looking at the instructions at all!

- First, fold your sheet in paper (fig 1) diagonally, coloured side outwards, so that it forms a triangle (fig 2)

- Next, fold each of the two corners at each end of the long edge up to the other corner to crease (fig 3), then fold them back down again (fig 4).

Step 2: Fold Petals Part 2

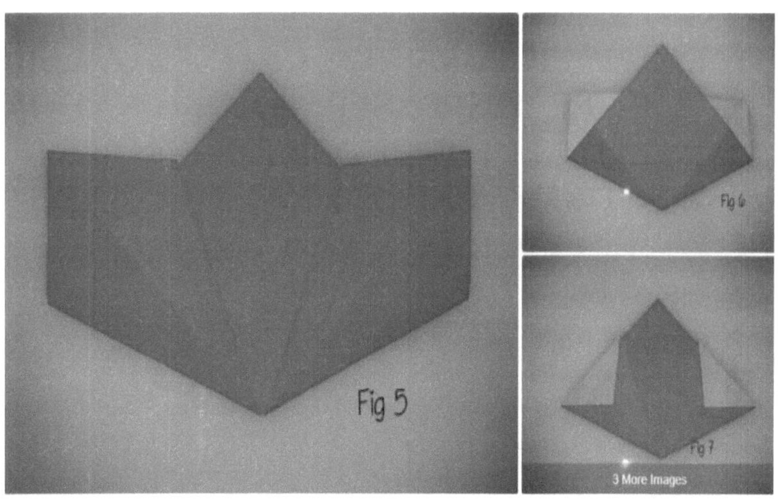

Fold one of the corners up at the crease you just made, and squash it down so that what was the edge runs along the centre of the flap, on top of the crease. Do the same with the other corner, so that it looks like fig 5 from the front and fig 6 from the back.

- Can you see the white parts peeking out where you have just folded? You want to fold these down. You can tuck them in, so that the white can't be seen, org you can fold them outwards like we have in fig 7. We like the white part, as it adds contrast to the colour!

- Next, fold the two flaps inwards as we have in fig 8. Run some glue down one side of the flap (fig 9) and press the two flaps together to create a petal (fig 10). Secure with a clothes peg while the glue dries!

NOTE: IN THE PICTURE, YOU CAN SEE US USING A GLUE TAPE DISPENSER. WE really DON'T RECOMMEND GLUE TAPE FOR THIS PROJECT - IT JUST ISN'T STRONG ENOUGH! WE LEARNED THE HARD WAY, SO YOU DON'T HAVE TO ;-)

Step 3: Create Flowers...

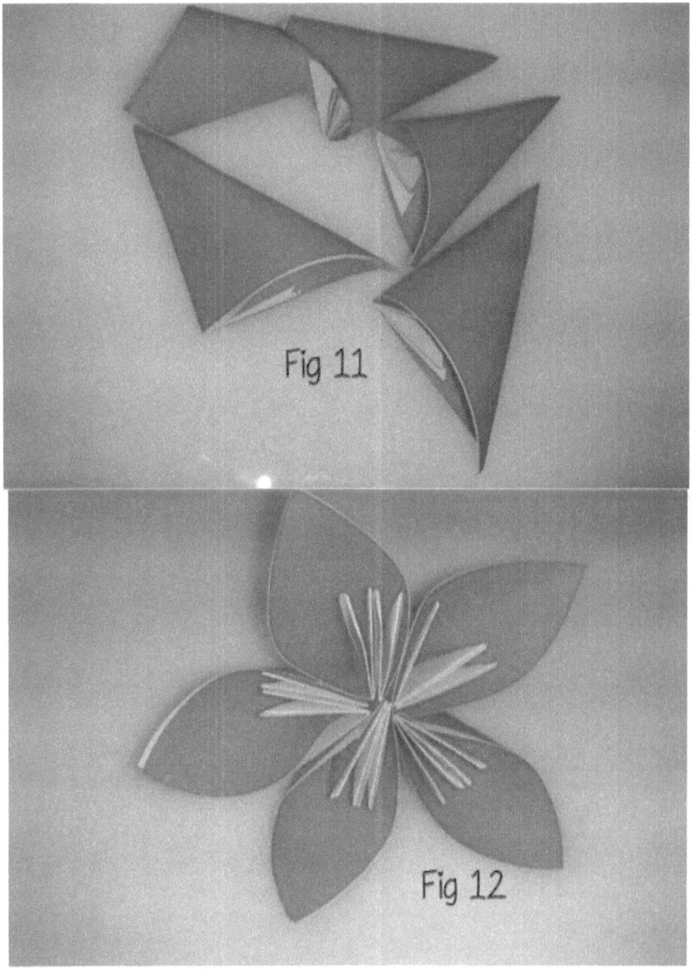

Fig 11

Fig 12

- Repeat the previous two steps a further four times, using the same colour of paper. By the time you have done this you will be a pro, and probably won't even need to look at the instructions to follow each step any more!

- Once you have done that (fig 11) you are ready to build your first flower. Run a small amount of glue along the edge of each petal. Carefully place them together, using clothes pegs to secure. We found it easiest to glue the first four petals together, then once the glue is thoroughly dry, glue the fifth one into position.

Step 4: ...Lots of Flowers!

Fig 13

Fig 14

- Way to go! You created your first flower! I'm sure you can think of lots of ways to use these flowers as they are, but to create the flower ball, we need another 11 of them. We created 2 each in 6 rainbow colours, following the same steps each time. It sounds laborious, but you will get really quick at making them!

- Once you have done that, it is time to start gluing the individual flowers together. To do this, run a glue down the length of the spine of one petal each of three different coloured flowers. Press the three spines together so that the tips of the petal meet, and hold together with a clothes peg until the glue has dried. Repeat with the next petal along, so that each flower ends up attached to one flower of each of the other colours by two petals each. Don't be tempted to glue too many at a time, especially once the ball starts to build up - the flowers will require quite a bit of pressure to hold into place, and the more areas where the glue is still wet, the harder that is to do.

- It can be hard work visualising what colour goes where - I would suggest by attaching each of the other colours round one central flower, then checking what goes where by figuring out which colour is immediately opposite in the ball, and making sure you place the same colour. This can be a very good exercise in visualisation! Depending on your company, it can also lead to all types of questions - first about colour itself, then about colour perception, whether we all perceive colour the same way, and how we even know that (an incredibly worthwhile and valuable conversation!)

- During this time, your ball may look a bit of a mess - mine certainly did, as you can see in fig 14! Don't be disheartened, it will look like this right up until the last flower is glued in place, but then it will all come together, I promise ;-)

Step 5: Hanging Your Finished Kusudama Ball

- You don't have to hang your ball if you don't want to. It would make a great decoration as it is, or you could attach it to a dowel to make it stand like a flower, but we chose to make a mobile to hang. All you need to do is punch a hole in one corner of a flower, loop with some ribbon or string, and hang!

Modular Origami Seasonal Ornament

This is a type of modular origami kusudama made into an ornament....called a star sea, I am not sure who the original author of this particular fold is. I hope you enjoy this tutorial. This modular origami is put together with both glue and tape (on the inside of module) for stability as they will be used as ornaments, which will be "handled" from time to time. This is a type of modular origami kusudama made into an ornament....called a star sea, I am not sure who the original author of this particular fold is. I hope you enjoy this tutorial. This modular origami is put together with both glue and tape (on the inside of module) for stability as they will be used as ornaments, which will be "handled" from time to time.

You Will Need

- Origami Paper
- Coloured
- Foil Glue
- Stick
- <u>Tape</u>

Instruction

Step 1

You will need 12 pieces of square paper measuring 3 inches by 3 inches each.

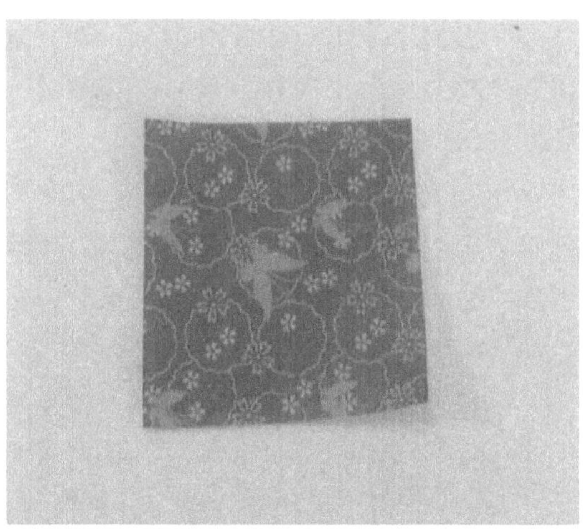

Step 2

Take the first piece of paper and fold it in half....then unfold.

Take one side of the paper, and fold up to the center crease that you just made in step 1 (shown here). Repeat this step on the other side.

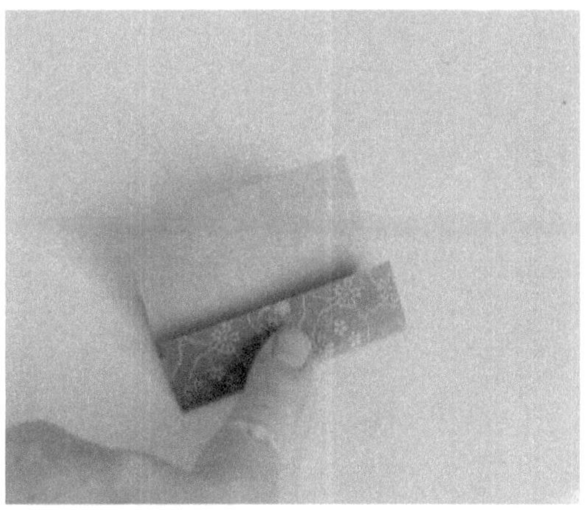

This is what you should have so far....

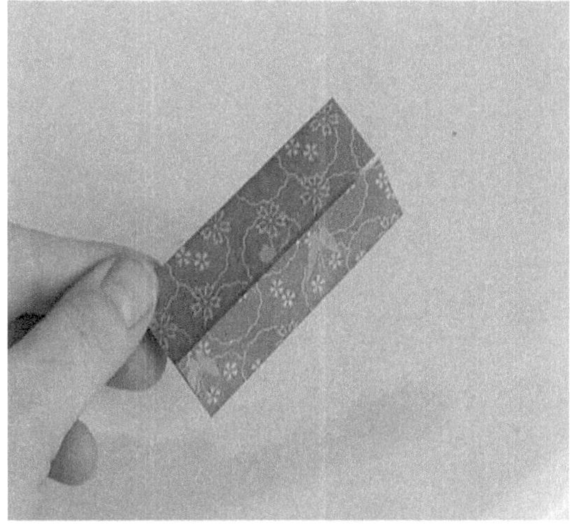

Take the top left hand corner of the module and fold down until it's flush (shown here). Crease.

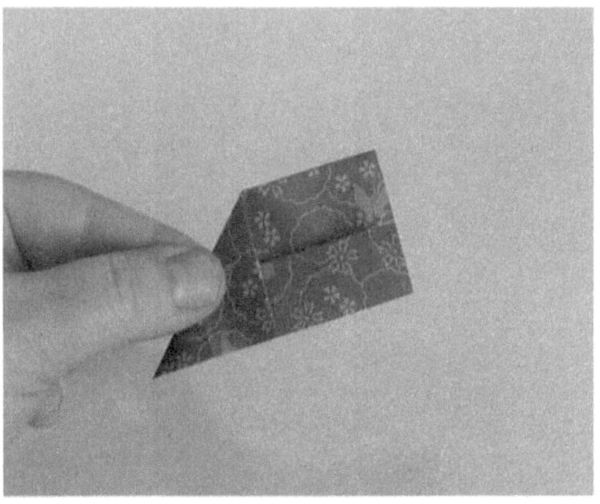

Take the bottom right corner (shown in step 5), and bring the corner up to meet the triangle shape created in step 5....shown here. Crease. This is what your module should look like now.

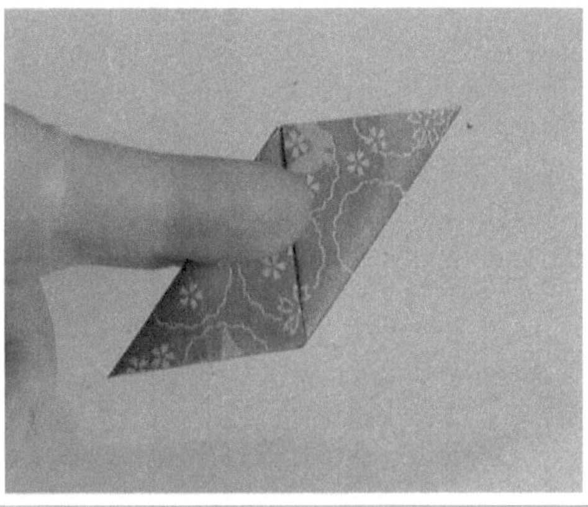

Now...unfold....This is what the crease marks look like. Turn the module over.....

This is the back of the module. Repeat steps 5 and 6 on this side....

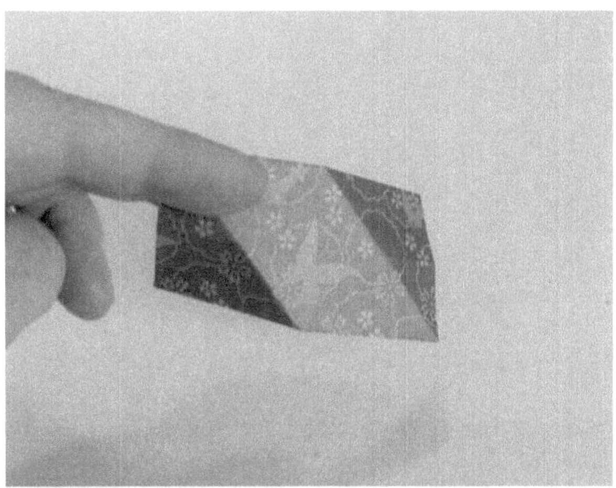

....First corner...fold down as before...

...bring the other corner up, just as before, and crease.

When you unfold the two triangle folds, you will see two (x) patterns shown here....Fold the module back on itself...in half...(shown in next step)

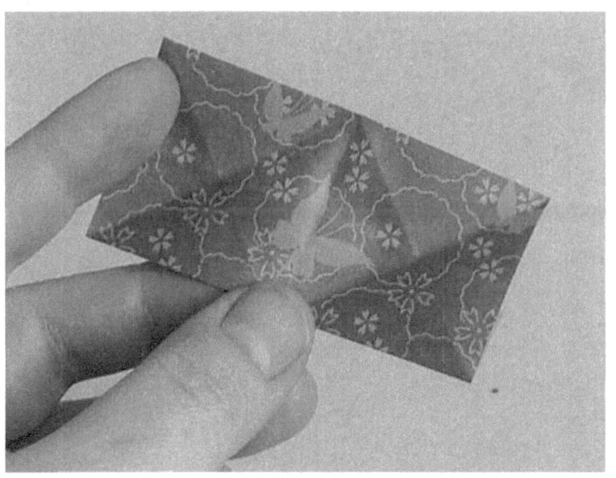

Like...this...Crease.

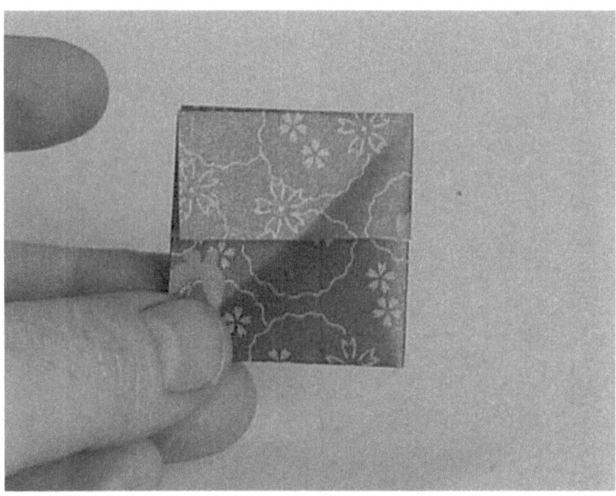

The crease just made creates a separation line between the two (x's) shown here.

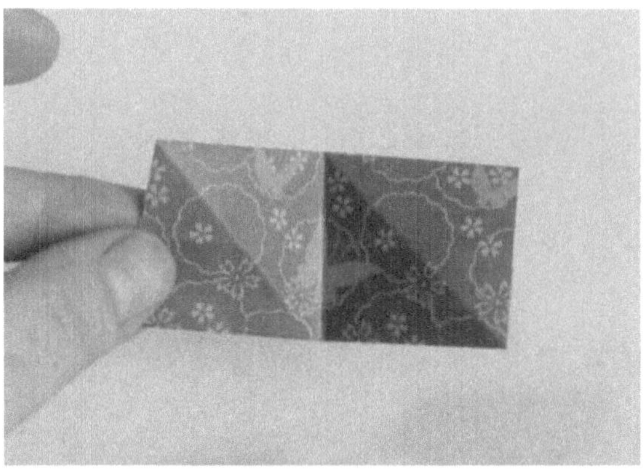

Take the left side of the module, and bring toward the center line....then crease it. Do the same for the right hand side. This will place vertical line down the center of each (x).

Look closely at this picture. We are going to make a small (v) crease in the top part of the first "x" shown here.

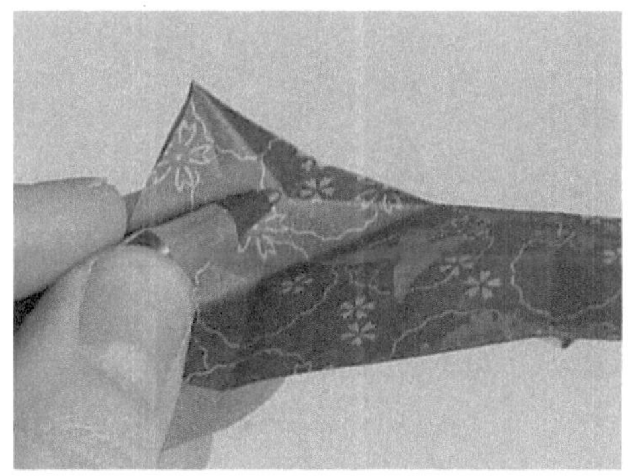

Once you've made the small "v" crease, we are slowly going to fold the left side towards the center line of the module....You will notice how the "v" fold is tucking in....

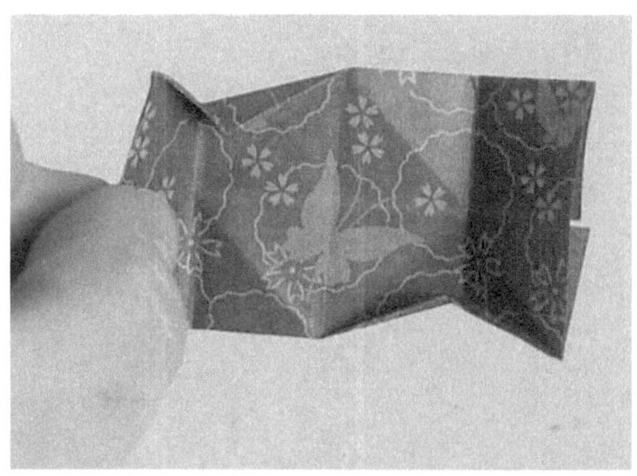

....keep closing...

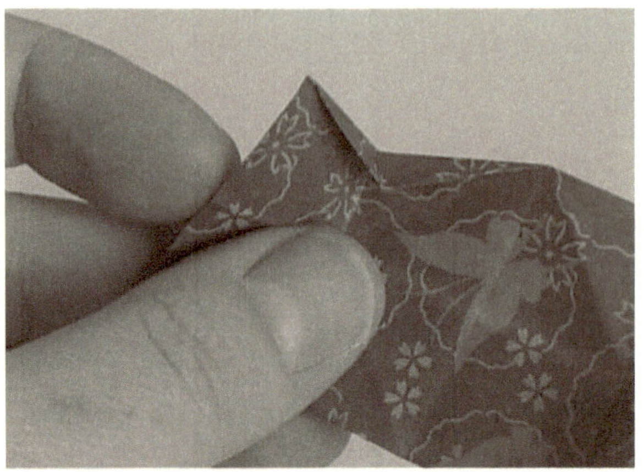

...and it's closed.....repeat the process on the other side EXCEPT, create that small "v" crease on the opposite end of the module. Then fold in as before. Look at step 19.

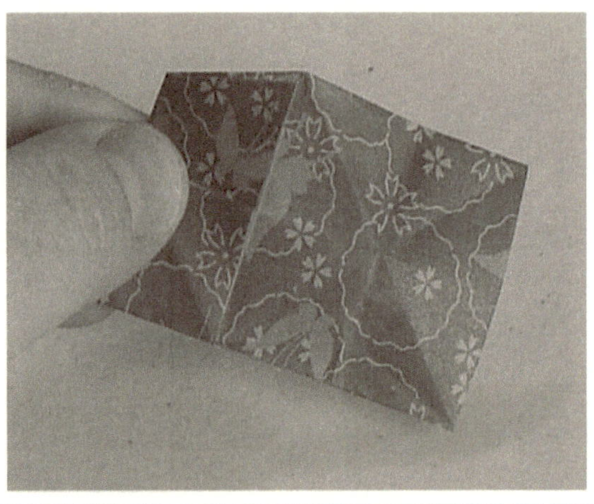

Ok! This is what your module looks like now! Unfold the two flaps gently....

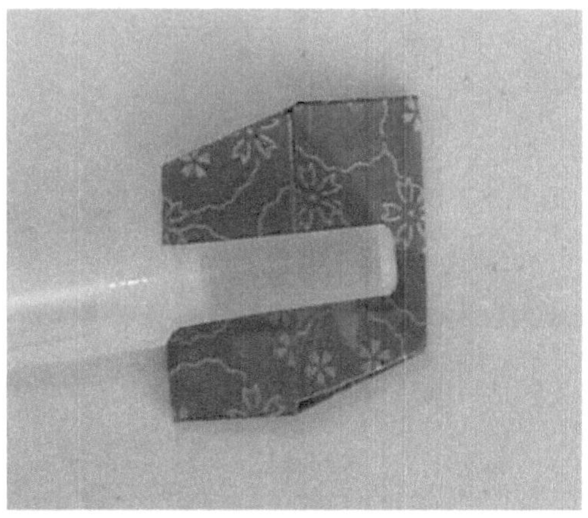

Now, bring the top left corner down to the bottom-center of the module...shown here. Then bring the bottom right corner up to the top-center. See next step.

Wonderful! You have completed the module. You must have a total of 12 modules to make the ornament.

You can create more sparkle to your module by inserting and glueing a piece of square foil to the framed center of the module. (optional)

As you can see here, I've just glued the insert in....

This is what the finished module looks like. Make 12 of them, and then we will put the whole thing together.

Ok...lets put together....

If you look at the modules here, you will notice that there are "tabs" on either side of each module, and on the back of it, there are "pockets".

Turn two pieces over on their backsides....insert "tab" of one module into one of the "pockets" in the other module...shown here. Add a tiny piece of tape for stability.

When you turn the two modules over, they should look like this so far.

So far, you have taken module 2 "tab", and placed into module 1 pocket. Now place module 1 "tab" into a module 3 pocket shown here. Add a wee bit of tape to stabalize.

This is what you should have so far...now we are going to join all three together as a starting unit for the completed ornament....view next step.

Join the three modules together by tucking module 3 "tab" into module 1 pocket. We want to create a "hollow" triangle effect on the inside. View below.

This is what the inside starting ring looks like! Here is what it looks like on the outside....next step please!

This is how it looks on the outside. AND this is the 3 ring unit that we build upon. Only 9 more modules to attach! This module is made up of 3 unit "TRIANGLES" seen here surrounded by a 4 piece "DIAMONDS" or "STARS" pattern. Look at the next step.

This is the "STAR" or "DIAMOND" pattern that surrounds the "TRIANGLE" units. This will help you create the ornament....

Step 35

Turn module over to the back again....grab another module, (module four), and insert "tab" into the side pocket of the triangle shown here. Add a bit of tape. Now...grab another module (module 5), and insert "tab" into another inside pocket of the hollow triangle. Grab another module, (module 6), and insert "tab" into another open pocket of the hollow triangle....

This is what it looks like now from the front. The modules that you just added (4,5,6) are the longest points of the module shown here. Turn back over....

When you turn model over you will see the 3 longer points (just created by adding modules 4,5,6)and three short "tab" points. The short points are where you will insert modules 7,8 and 9 onto. Secure with a bit of tape.

Okay, this is what your modules look like from the back so far. Now you have the means to create 3 more "hollow triangles" by tucking in the shorter "tabs" into the nearby pockets. Again, secure with a bit of tape.

Here, we are creating the second "hollow triangle.....continue around the model in this manner....

This is what your model looks like now. It has a total of 4 hallow triangles. Add modules 10,11,12 into the open side pockets of the surrounding hallow triangles. Insert the shorter surrounding "tabs" into 10,11,12 pockets, and secure with a bit of tape. Continue in this manner until the ball is closed, and your done!

Step 41

The best way to understand this tutorial is to follow along with your modules as you read the tutorial. If you just scan the directions without the modules in hand, then you will find this quite difficult....so make the modules first, and then proceed....